Publisher's Note

The drawings in this coloring book illustrate the amazing history of flight, beginning with Leonardo's design for a flying machine 500 years ago, continuing with the first actual human ascent in a balloon, and proceeding through a mind-boggling array of balloons, dirigibles, gliders, airplanes, a helicopter, and rocket-powered spacecraft, to the present day. Pictured are many famous flying machines, like the Wright brothers' first airplane—and many less well known but still notable machines, like the dirigible *R34* and the Boeing 40A mail plane. Together, the drawings present significant high points in the thrilling, truly unique history of the human attempt to fly.

There are two fundamentally different kinds of man-made flying machines: lighter-than-air craft and heavier-than-air craft. Balloons make use of lighter-than-air gases (or air that has been heated to make it lighter than the air around it) to achieve lift. A *dirigible* (or *airship*; *blimp* is a more recent term for a certain type of dirigible) is a balloon equipped with mechanical driving power and an apparatus for steering so that it is not at the mercy of every gust of wind. Lighter-than-air flying devices are still frequently seen and are even increasing in popularity. The most important flying machines from a historical perspective, however, are clearly the heavier-than-air machines. These include gliders, helicopters, and, most important of all, airplanes. What most of these various devices have in common is that they use the flow of air over a specially shaped surface to provide the lift. The major exception is the rocket ship (designed primarily for flight into regions where there is little or no air), which uses the sheer force of thrust alone to counteract the pull of gravity.

Most of the heavier-than-air flight vehicles in this book are airplanes. The four basic forces affecting airplane flight are shown in Figure 1. Figure 2, illustrating the principle of lift, shows the cross section of a wing passing through the air.

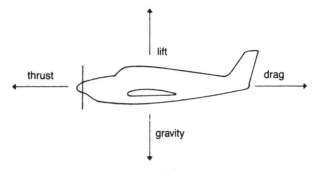

FIG. 1. Forces Affecting Flight

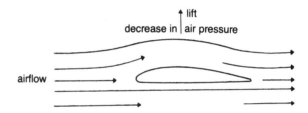

FIG. 2. The Principle of Lift

The curved upper surface of the wing causes the air on that side to flow faster than the air on the underside of the wing. According to a law of physics first described in 1738 by the Swiss scientist Daniel Bernoulli, the faster a fluid (such as air) flows, the less pressure it exerts on its surroundings. Therefore the faster-flowing air on top of the wing creates a lower-pressure area on that side, causing the relatively high pressure below to *lift* the wing. This scientific principle is operative in all heavier-than-air craft that use wings to counteract the force of gravity. That naturally includes all of the successful airplanes illustrated in this book, no matter how strange they may appear!

The centerfold drawing, showing the Boeing 707 jet airliner, has been placed out of chronological order, since it also serves to illustrate the parts of an airplane.

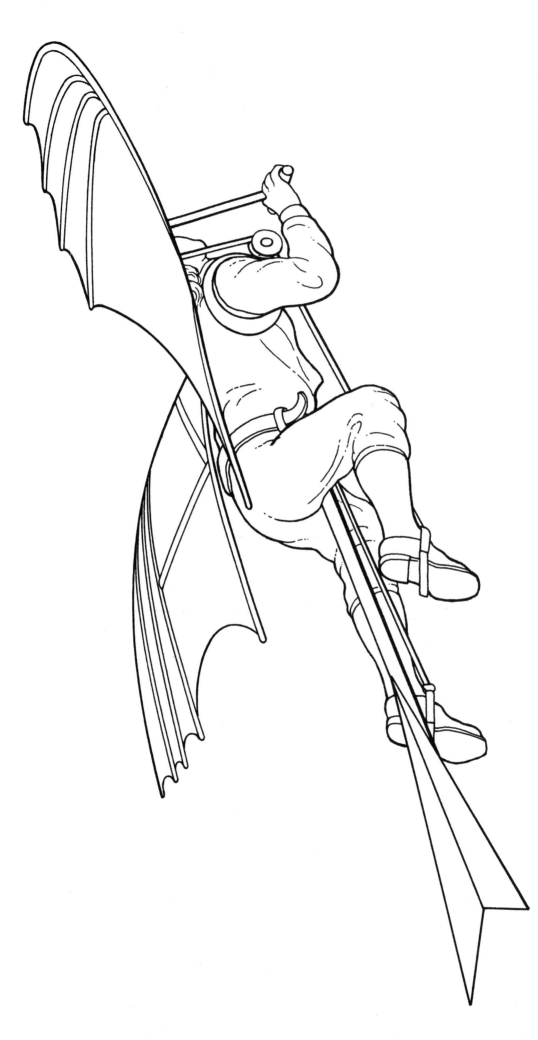

1. Leonardo da Vinci Ornithopter. This design for a man-powered ornithopter (wing-flapping aircraft) was developed around 1485. Leonardo also invented the parachute and designed a vertical takeoff device powered by a spring mechanism. These designs were far in advance of their time, but were not sufficiently developed for practical application.

History of Flight

Coloring Book

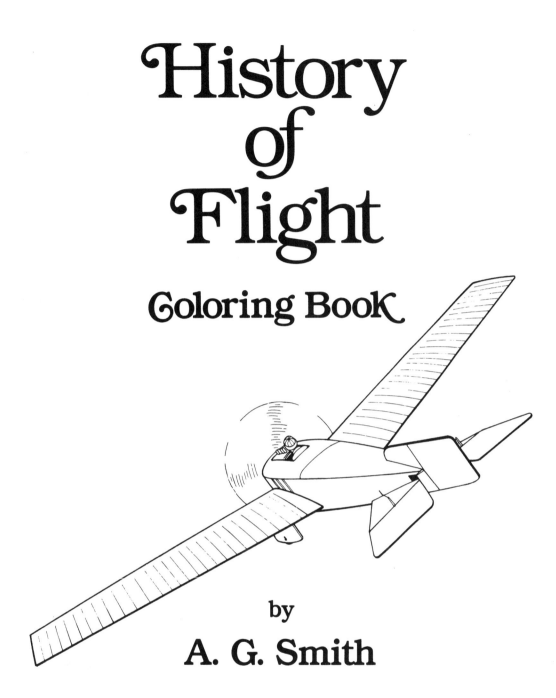

by

A. G. Smith

Dover Publications, Inc.
New York

For
Captain A. M. Wynne, Jr.

Published in Canada by General Publishing Company, Ltd., 30
Lesmill Road, Don Mills, Toronto, Ontario.
Published in the United Kingdom by Constable and Company,
Ltd., 10 Orange Street, London WC2H 7EG.

History of Flight Coloring Book is a new work, first published by
Dover Publications, Inc., in 1986.

DOVER *Pictorial Archive* SERIES

This book belongs to the Dover Pictorial Archive Series. You
may use the designs and illustrations for graphics and crafts
applications, free and without special permission, provided that
you include no more than ten in the same publication or project.
(For permission for additional use, please write to Dover Publications, Inc., 31 East 2nd Street, Mineola, N.Y. 11501.)
Republication or reproduction of any illustrations by any other
graphics service in any book or in any other design resource is
strictly prohibited.

International Standard Book Number: 0-486-25244-2

Manufactured in the United States of America
Dover Publications, Inc., 31 East 2nd Street, Mineola, N.Y.
11501

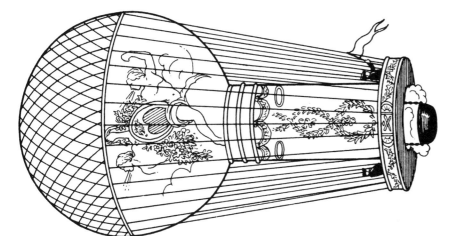

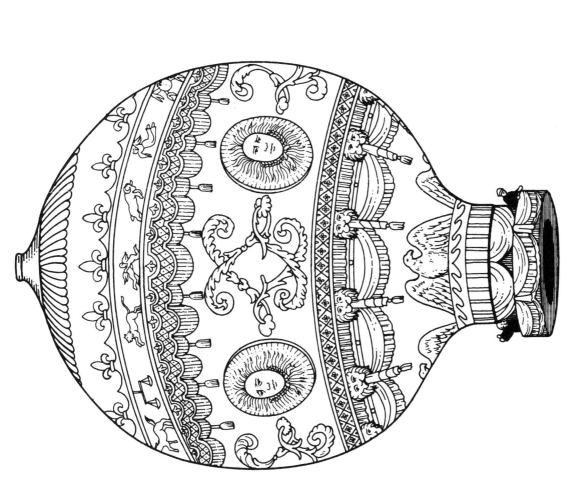

2. Early French Balloons. In 1783 both the hot-air and hydrogen-filled balloons were developed in France. The hot-air balloon, designed by Joseph and Étienne Montgolfier, made its first free flight with passengers over Paris on November 21, 1783 (left). The following month, the first hydrogen-filled balloon, designed and manned by Professor J.-A.-C. Charles, also made its first successful ascent. In 1785, **Pilâtre de Rozier** (the first human ever to have ascended in a balloon) and P.-A. de Romain crashed while attempting to fly the English Channel in a balloon (right) combining hot air and hydrogen—a dangerous combination.

3. Cayley's "Convertiplane." Sir George Cayley (1773–1857), "the father of British aeronautics" and one of the great geniuses in the history of flight design, published this helicopter design in 1843. The "convertiplane" consisted of four rotating sets of blades for lifting and two pusher propellers for forward motion. In 1804, Cayley had designed a small model glider that flew, the first ever to have embodied the structure of the fixed-wing airplane as we know it today.

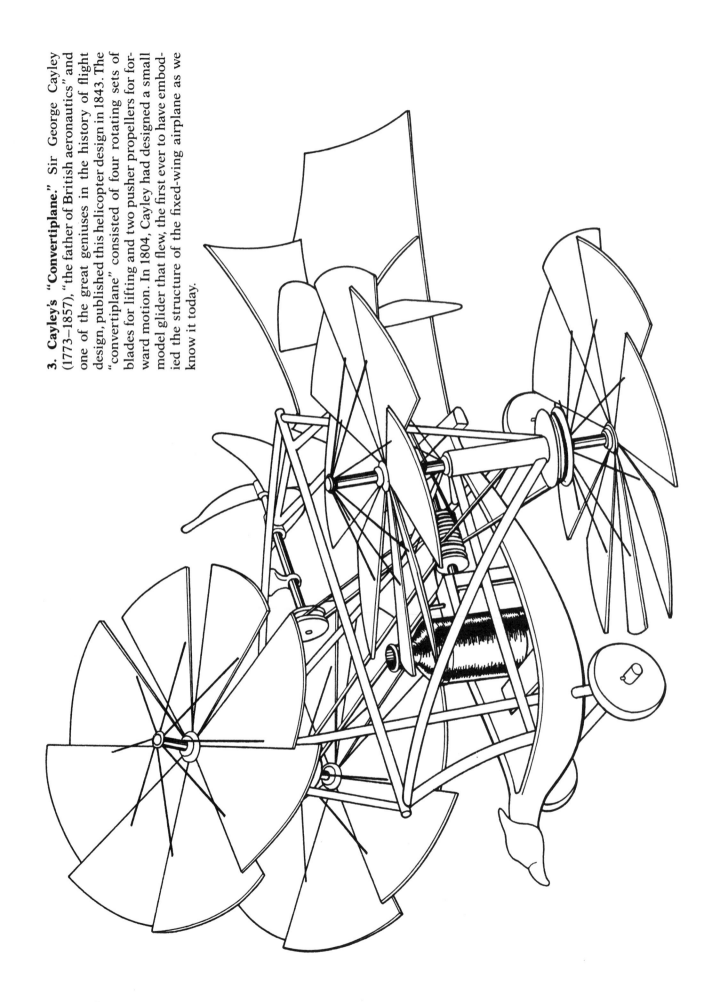

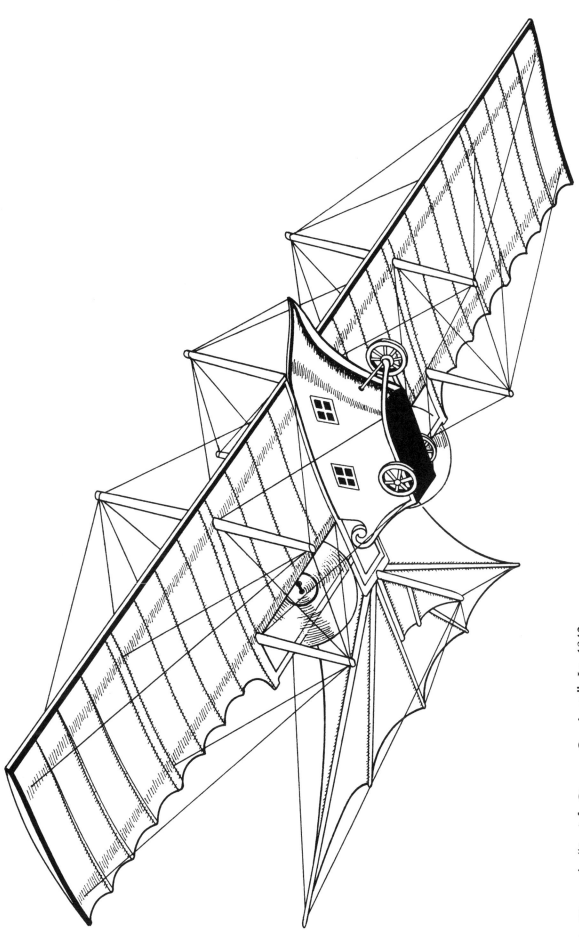

4. Henson's "Aerial Steam Carriage." In 1842, William Henson produced the first design for a complete powered airplane. In 1848, his partner and fellow enthusiast John Stringfellow modified Henson's designs to build a steam-powered model that flew for a short distance.

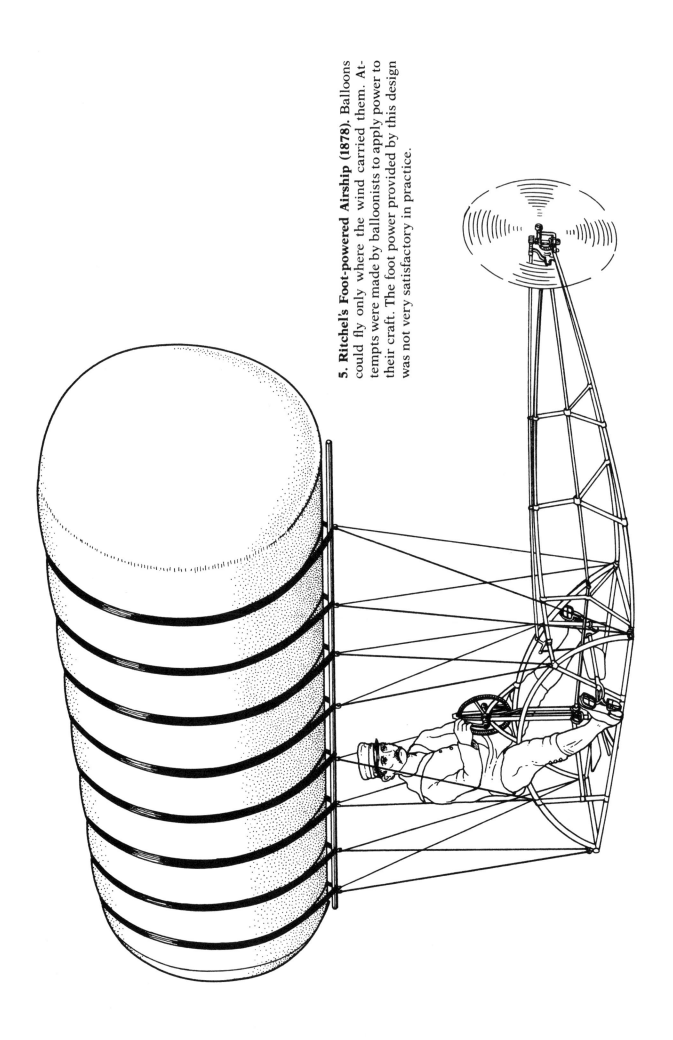

5. Ritchel's Foot-powered Airship (1878). Balloons could fly only where the wind carried them. Attempts were made by balloonists to apply power to their craft. The foot power provided by this design was not very satisfactory in practice.

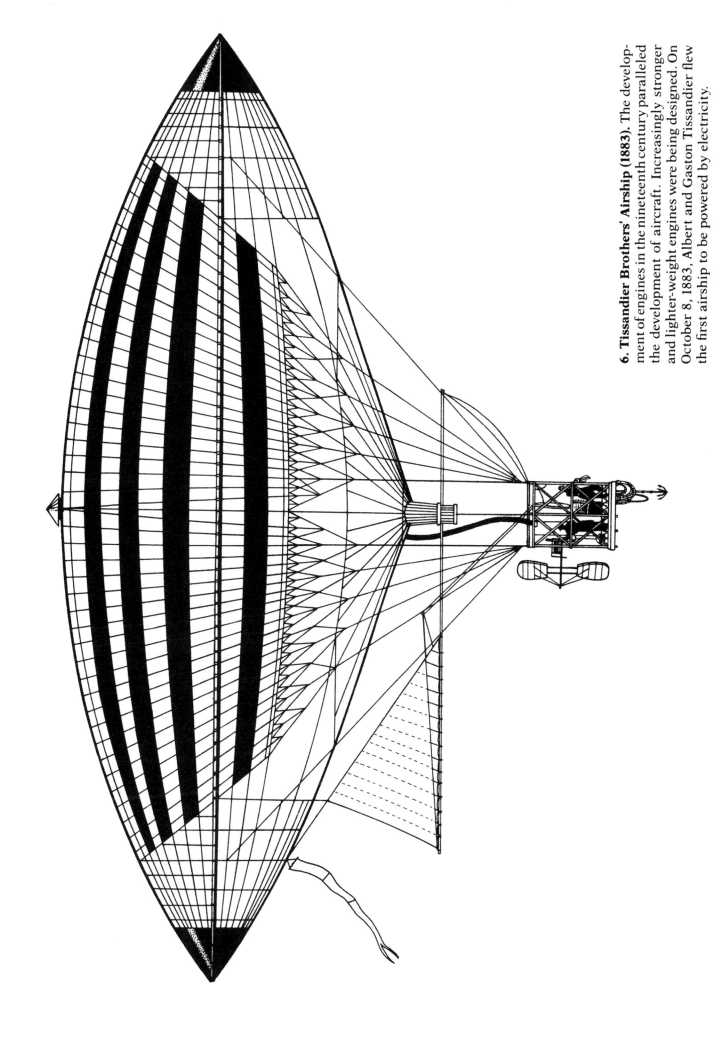

6. Tissandier Brothers' Airship (1883). The development of engines in the nineteenth century paralleled the development of aircraft. Increasingly stronger and lighter-weight engines were being designed. On October 8, 1883, Albert and Gaston Tissandier flew the first airship to be powered by electricity.

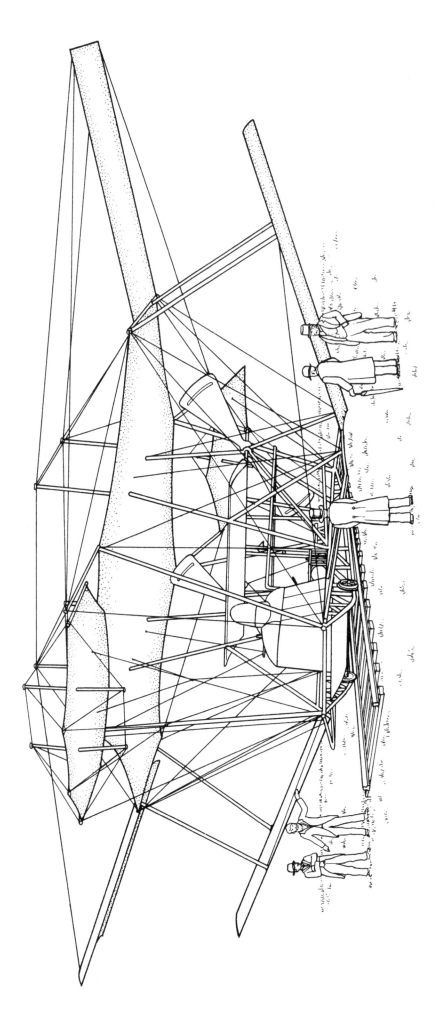

7. Maxim's Giant (1894). This enormous machine had a wingspan of 104 feet and weighed 3½ tons. It was powered by two 180 hp. steam engines. It actually lifted itself off the ground but was uncontrolla-ble. Sir Hiram Stevens Maxim (1840–1916) was one of many inventors who tried to achieve heavier-than-air flight by brute force.

8. Lilienthal's Biplane Glider (1895). Between 1891 and his death in an air accident in 1896, Otto Lilienthal (b. 1848), the German aviator and first successful glider pilot, made more than 2,000 successful glider flights. One of the "birdmen-scientists" who knew that in order for man to fly he must first understand the principles of flight, Lilienthal had a profound influence on the development of practical aircraft.

9. Chanute's Biplane Glider (1896). Lilienthal's disciples Octave Chanute (1832–1910) in America and Percy Pilcher (1866–1899) in Britain continued his work. Chanute's biplane glider employed the same truss rigging that the Wrights were to use in their early biplane structures. This craft had a 16-foot wingspan.

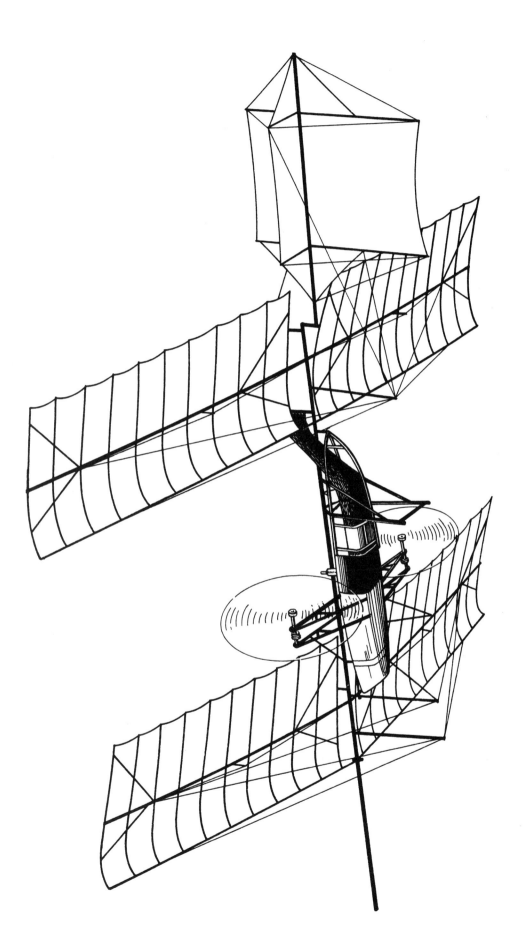

10. Langley's *Aerodrome Number 5* (1896). Professor Samuel Pierpont Langley (1834–1906), Secretary of the Smithsonian Institution in Washington, was a distinguished American scientist and a pioneer in the development of powered heavier-than-air flying machines. In the 1880s he began experimenting with small-scale models powered by rubber bands. His later models had tandem wings and were powered by steam engines. On May 6, 1896, his steam-driven *Aerodrome Number 5* was launched from a catapult in the Potomac River and made two flights, of 3,200 feet and 2,300 feet respectively. Langley's *Aerodrome Number 5* had a wingspan of 13 feet 8 inches and was the first really successful powered airplane, although still not a man-carrying machine.

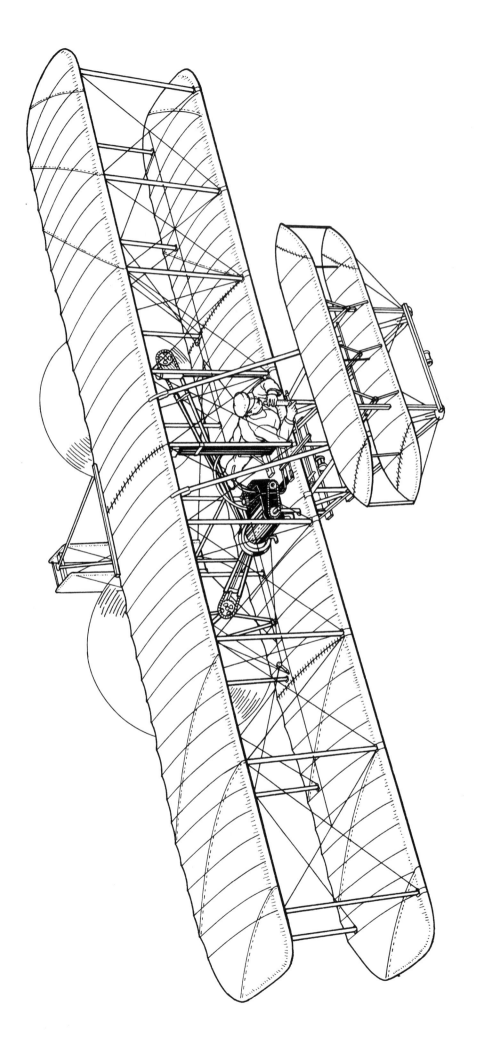

11. Wright Brothers' *Flyer* (1903). The first sustained, controlled, human-carrying flight by a powered heavier-than-air craft was made on December 17, 1903, at Kill Devil Hill, near Kitty Hawk, North Carolina. Both the engine and the airplane were designed by the American brothers Wilbur and Orville Wright (1867–1912; 1871–1948). The original *Flyer*, first flown by Orville, had a wingspan of 40 feet 4 inches and was 21 feet long. The four-cylinder internal-combustion engine was rated at 8–12 hp.

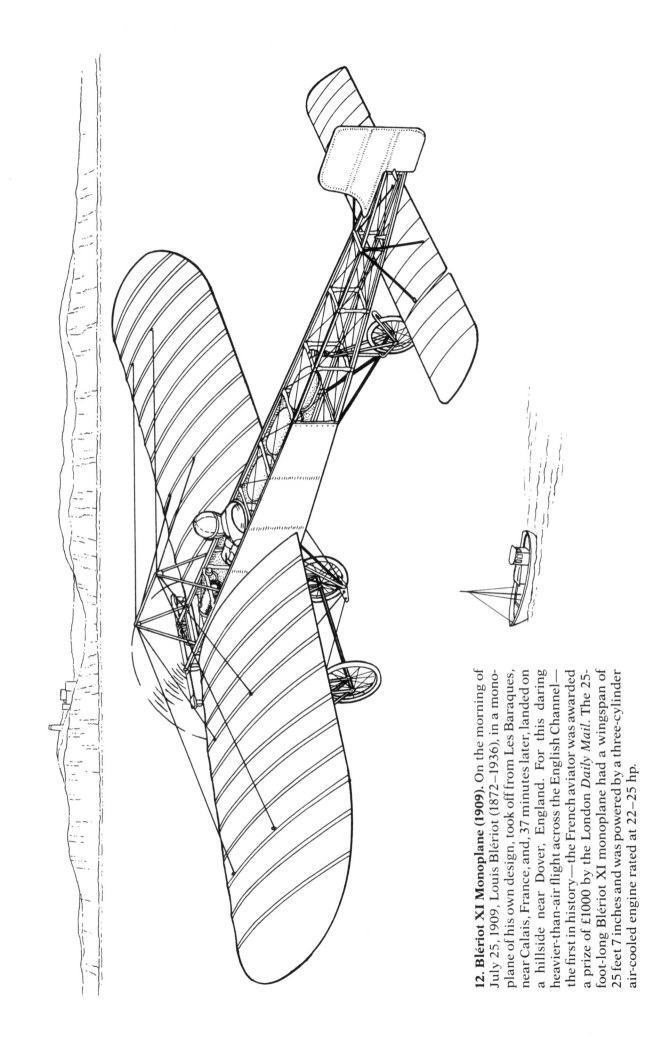

12. Blériot XI Monoplane (1909). On the morning of July 25, 1909, Louis Blériot (1872–1936), in a monoplane of his own design, took off from Les Baraques, near Calais, France, and, 37 minutes later, landed on a hillside near Dover, England. For this daring heavier-than-air flight across the English Channel—the first in history—the French aviator was awarded a prize of £1000 by the London *Daily Mail*. The 25-foot-long Blériot XI monoplane had a wingspan of 25 feet 7 inches and was powered by a three-cylinder air-cooled engine rated at 22–25 hp.

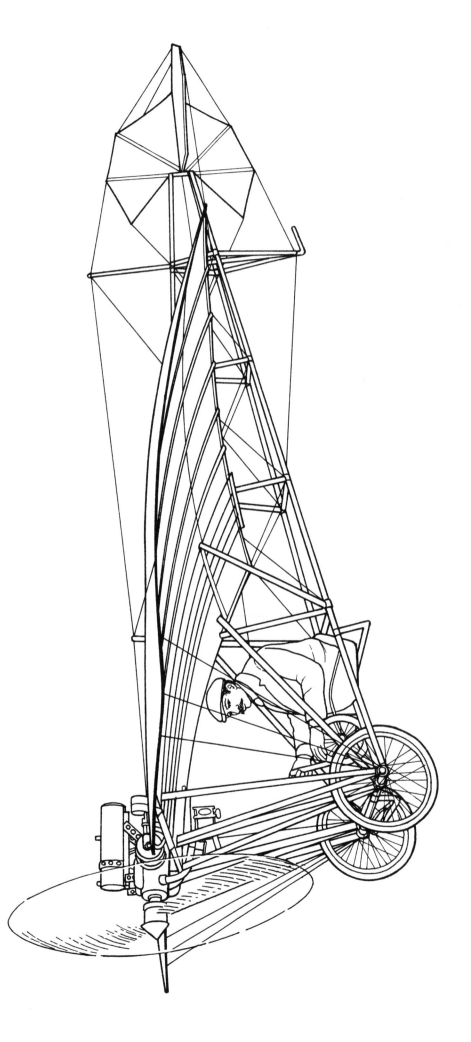

13. Santos-Dumont No. 20 _Demoiselle_ (1909). In France in 1909, the Brazilian Alberto Santos-Dumont (1873–1932), a noted figure in balloon and dirigible as well as heavier-than-air aviation, built and flew the world's first practical "light" airplane.

The No. 20 _Demoiselle_ ("Damselfly") had a wingspan of only 18 feet ½ inch and weighed only 242 pounds. Made of lightweight materials, mainly bamboo, wood, and linen, this machine inspired generations of "home-built" light planes.

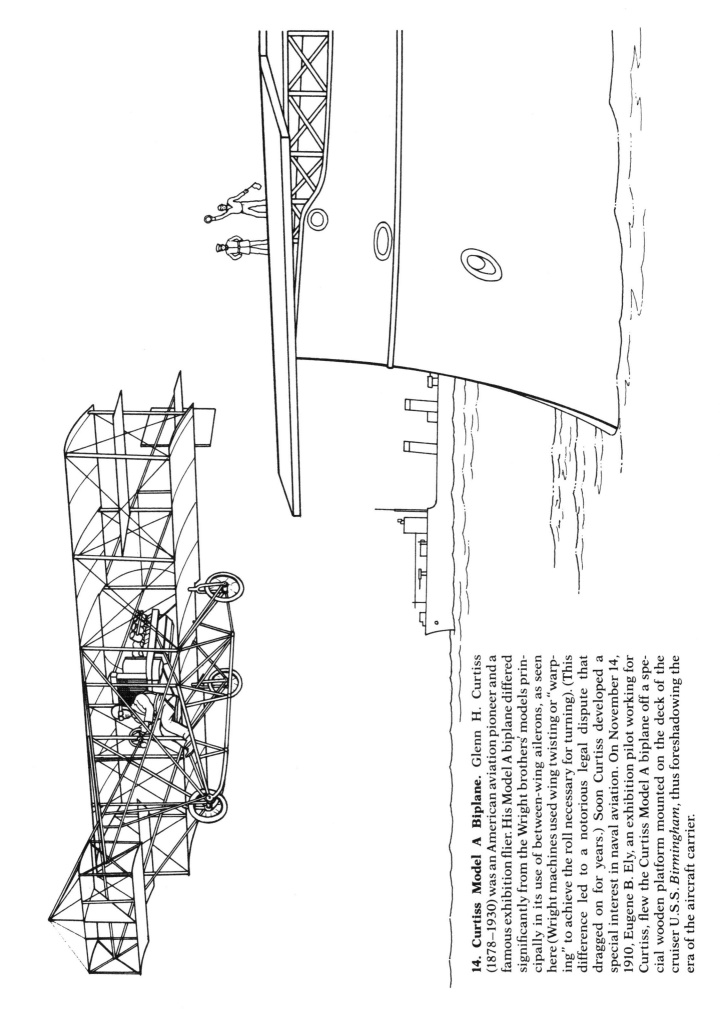

14. Curtiss Model A Biplane. Glenn H. Curtiss (1878–1930) was an American aviation pioneer and a famous exhibition flier. His Model A biplane differed significantly from the Wright brothers' models principally in its use of between-wing ailerons, as seen here (Wright machines used wing twisting or "warping" to achieve the roll necessary for turning). (This difference led to a notorious legal dispute that dragged on for years.) Soon Curtiss developed a special interest in naval aviation. On November 14, 1910, Eugene B. Ely, an exhibition pilot working for Curtiss, flew the Curtiss Model A biplane off of a special wooden platform mounted on the deck of the cruiser U.S.S. *Birmingham*, thus foreshadowing the era of the aircraft carrier.

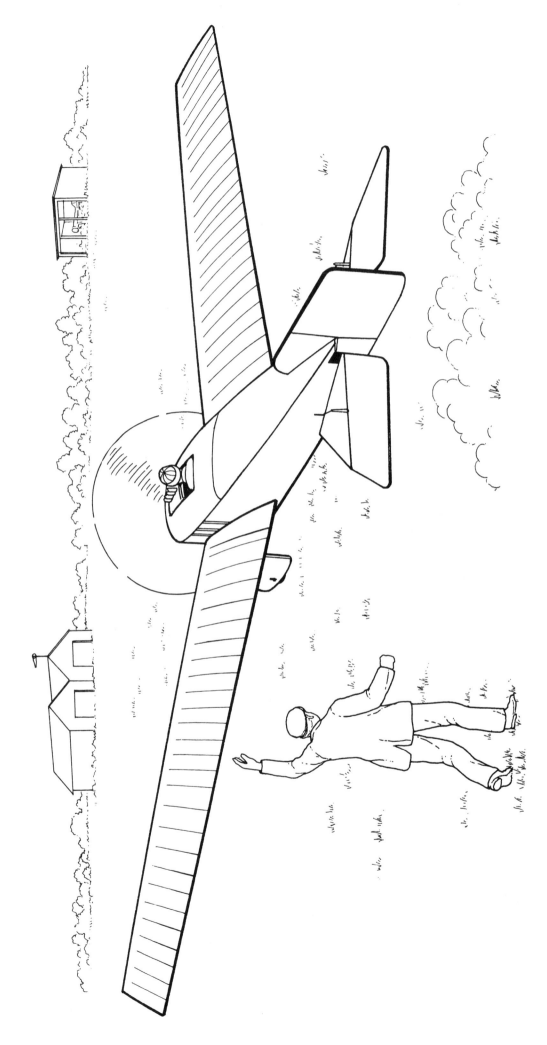

15. Experimental "Antoinette" (1911). The French engineer Léon Levavasseur (1863–1922) was a major contributor to monoplane design with his popular series of "Antoinette" airplanes. This 1911 "Antoinette" was experimental. With fully cantilevered wings and a single-piece, all-metal fuselage, its construction proved too heavy for its underpowered engine and the craft could make only a few short hops. Its innovative design features were successfully incorporated into later aircraft.

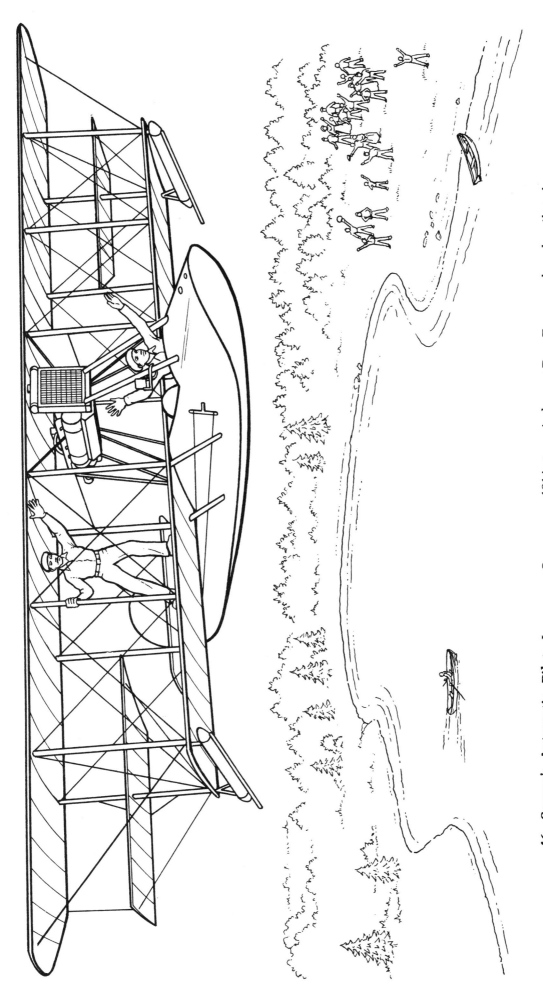

16. Sperry's Automatic Pilot. Lawrence Sperry (1892–1923) applied the gyroscopic stabilizer invented by his father, the famous American inventor Elmer A. Sperry (1860–1930), to the stabilization of aircraft, thus creating the first automatic pilot. The younger Sperry first demonstrated this device in 1914 at an airshow at Buc, France, where he piloted a Curtiss F flying boat. While aloft he held his hands in the air and his passenger stood on a wing, yet the plane flew steadily on without altering its course. He was awarded a substantial prize by the French government for this contribution to air safety.

17. Caproni CA46 Bomber. Italy was the first country to make bombing attacks from airplanes, in the Libyan (Italo-Turkish) War of 1911–12. Gianni Caproni built his first large bomber in 1913. Soon afterwards, during World War I, Caproni squadrons began heavy bombing raids against the Austrian enemy. The Caproni CA46 bomber had twin tail-booms and a central nacelle for the crew. Machine guns for protection against fighter planes were mounted in the nose and in a ring mount above the rear wing.

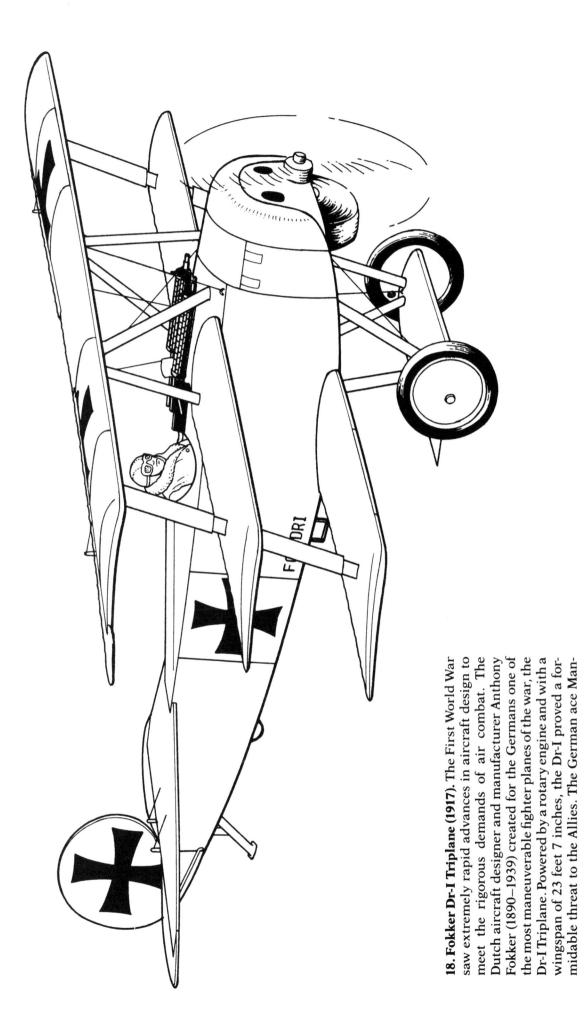

18. Fokker Dr-I Triplane (1917). The First World War saw extremely rapid advances in aircraft design to meet the rigorous demands of air combat. The Dutch aircraft designer and manufacturer Anthony Fokker (1890–1939) created for the Germans one of the most maneuverable fighter planes of the war, the Dr-I Triplane. Powered by a rotary engine and with a wingspan of 23 feet 7 inches, the Dr-I proved a formidable threat to the Allies. The German ace Manfred von Richthofen ("The Red Baron") was flying a Dr-I at the time of his death in 1918.

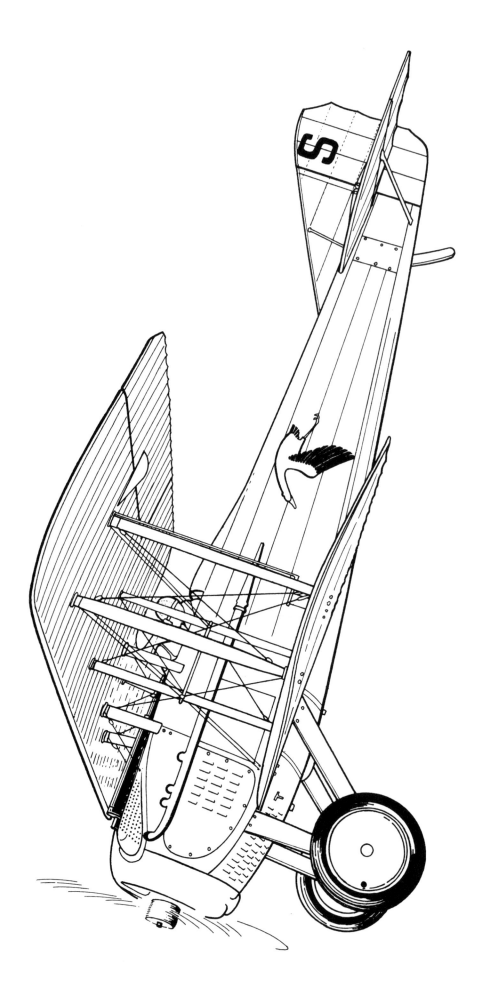

19. Spad 7. The French Spads (named after an acronym for the manufacturer, S.P.A.D., or "la Société Anonyme pour l'Aviation et ses Dérivés") were tough and powerful fighters of the later war years (1916–18), flown by both French and American squadrons. The honored French ace Captain Georges Guynemer piloted a Spad like the one shown here, while American ace Captain Eddie Rickenbacker achieved renown in a slightly later model. The Spad 7 was powered by a 180 hp. Hispano-Suiza engine.

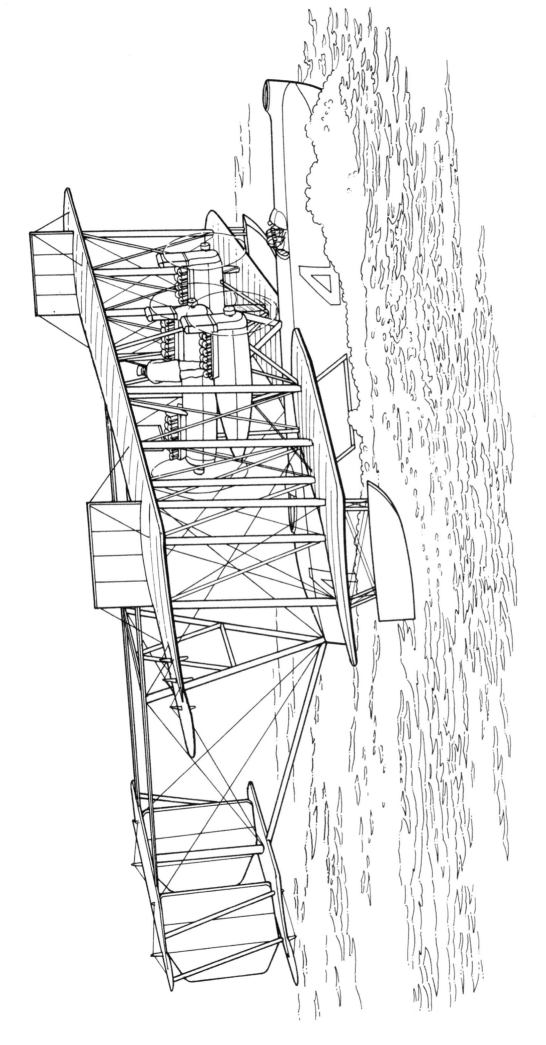

20. Curtiss Flying Boat *NC-4* (1919). After the war the great challenge to aviation became the crossing of the Atlantic Ocean. On May 8, 1919, three Curtiss flying boats designed for the Navy took off for Europe via Newfoundland, starting from Jamaica Bay, New York City. Two of the aircraft never made it past the Azores, but, after numerous delays and stops, the *NC-4*, with Lieutenant-Commander A. C. Read in charge and piloted by Walter Hinton, at last landed in Lisbon, Portugal, on May 27. (It reached Plymouth, England, on May 31.) Although not a non-stop flight, this had been the first successful trans-Atlantic crossing by air. Over 68 feet long, and with a wingspan of nearly 126 feet, the *NC-4* was a large plane for its day. It was powered by four engines of 400 hp. each.

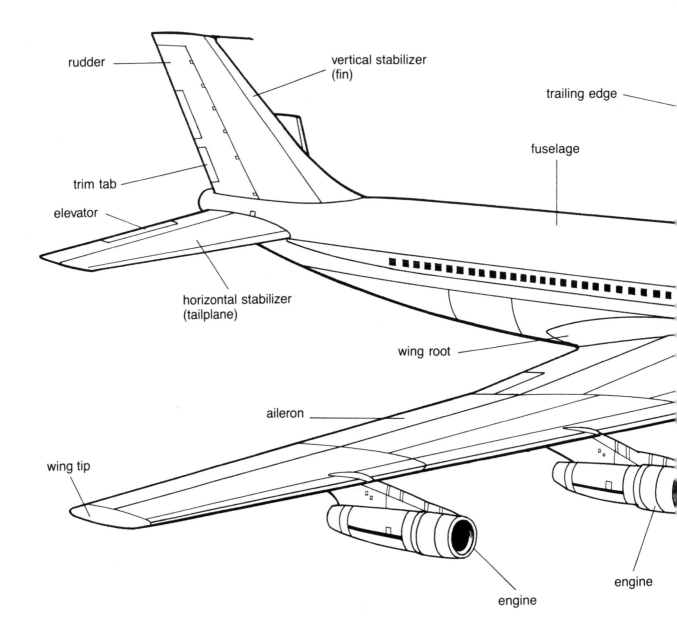

rudder

vertical stabilizer
(fin)

trailing edge

fuselage

trim tab

elevator

horizontal stabilizer
(tailplane)

wing root

aileron

wing tip

engine

engine

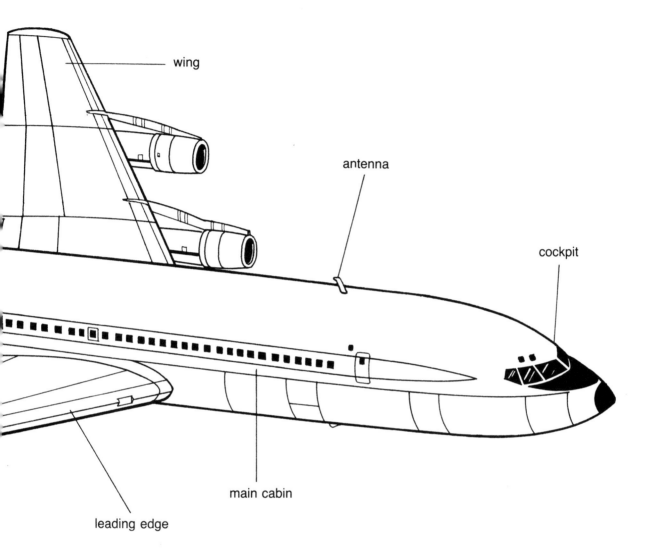

wing

antenna

cockpit

main cabin

leading edge

21. Boeing 707 (1954) Showing the Parts of an Airplane. The Boeing 707 was the first U.S. commercial jet airliner. The prototype first flew in 1954. The 707 went into regular service in 1958 and is still widely used on long-range routes. The wingspan of the 707 is 130 feet 10 inches and the plane is 144 feet 6 inches long. This drawing also illustrates the parts of an airplane.

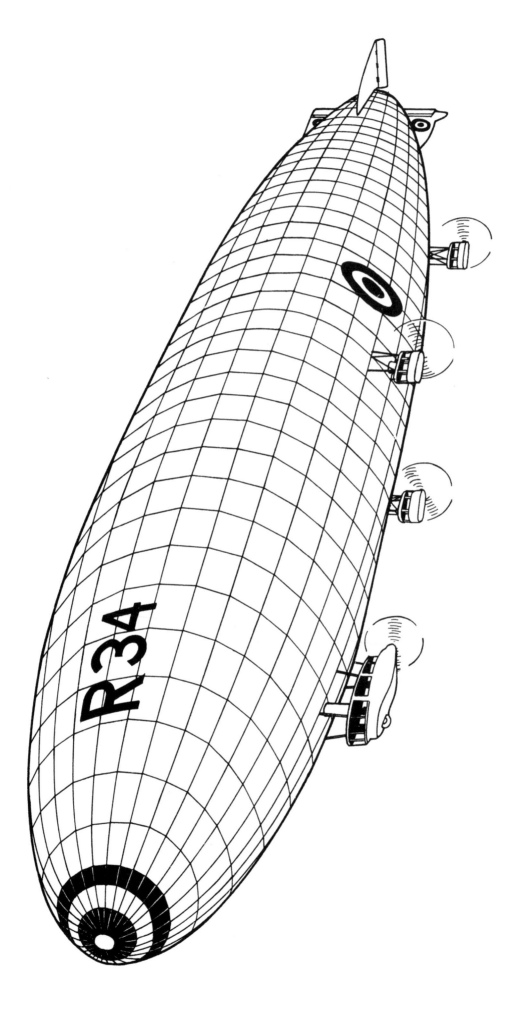

22. British Airship *R34* (1919). The first trans-Atlantic flight by a lighter-than-air vehicle was accomplished in July 1919, when the British airship *R34* made a round-trip crossing. The dirigible was commanded by Major G. H. Scott and it carried a crew of 31. The flight from Scotland to New York took 108 hours 12 minutes. The return flight to Pulham, Norfolk, took 75 hours 3 minutes. Dirigibles were used in commercial service during the late 1920s and the 1930s, but several disasters and the improvement of airplane technology led to their abandonment.

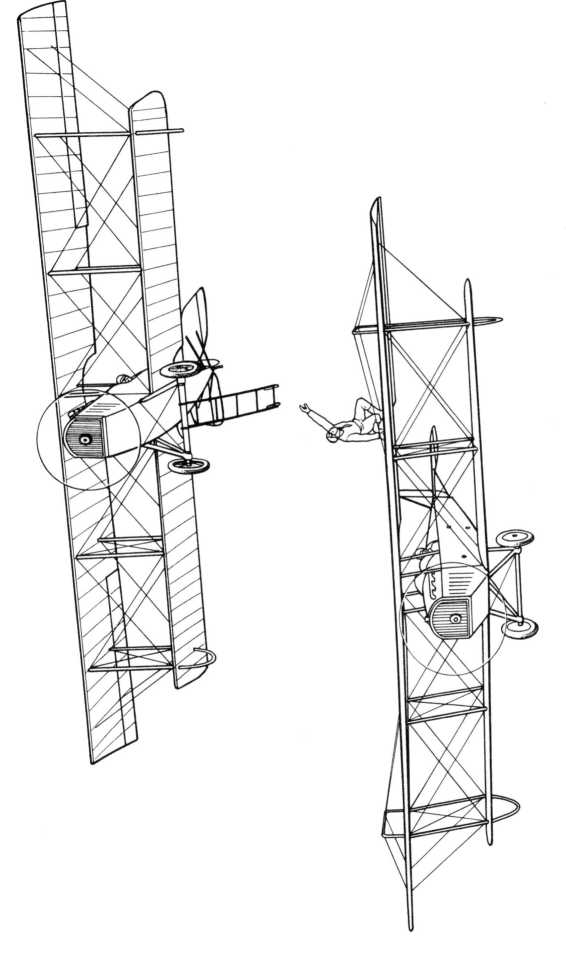

23. Curtiss JN-4 "Jenny." Another post-First-World-War phenomenon, especially in America, was "barnstorming." Ex-military pilots bought war-surplus aircraft and flew around the country earning a precarious living by giving exhibition flights, performing stunts, and selling rides. A favorite plane of the barnstormers was the Curtiss JN-4 "Jenny," originally built for war service as a two-seat training and reconnaissance plane. A reliable, cheap, and widely available biplane, the "Jenny" had an upper wingspan of 43 feet 7⅞ inches and was 27 feet 4 inches long. It could take off easily from rural pastures and be maintained by most mechanics.

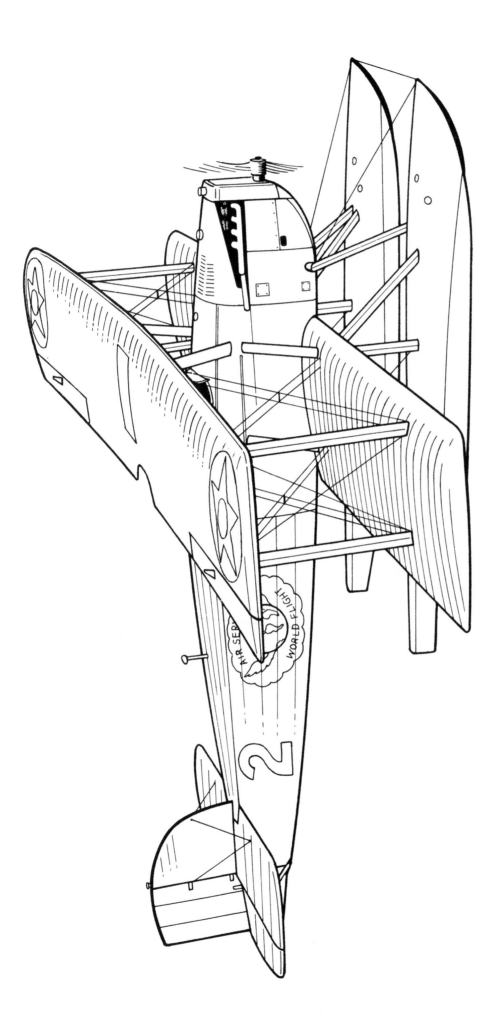

24. Douglas World Cruiser (1924). After the conquest of the Atlantic, the race was on to fly around the world. With this goal, four Douglas World Cruisers, named the *Seattle*, the *Chicago*, the *Boston*, and the *New Orleans*, took off from Seattle, heading west, on April 6, 1924. The *Seattle* crashed in Alaska (its crew was rescued) and much later the *Boston* went down in the Atlantic. After innumerable stops and difficulties, the *Chicago* and the *New Orleans*, as well as the *Boston II*, a replacement for the lost *Boston* manned by its crew, landed in Seattle on September 28, successfully completing a circuit of the globe covering over 26,000 miles. The sturdy Douglas World Cruiser was designed so that its pontoons could be readily replaced by wheels, and vice versa. It had a wingspan of 50 feet, a length of 35 feet 2½ inches.

25. Boeing 40A. The Boeing 40A was one of the first planes to be built specifically for the purpose of carrying mail, shortly after the U.S. government put the airmail service in the hands of private contractors in 1925. These planes were also among the first to carry paying long-distance passengers on a regular basis, leading eventually to modern commercial airline service. The Boeing 40A featured an enclosed, heated cabin that could carry several passengers as well as mail.

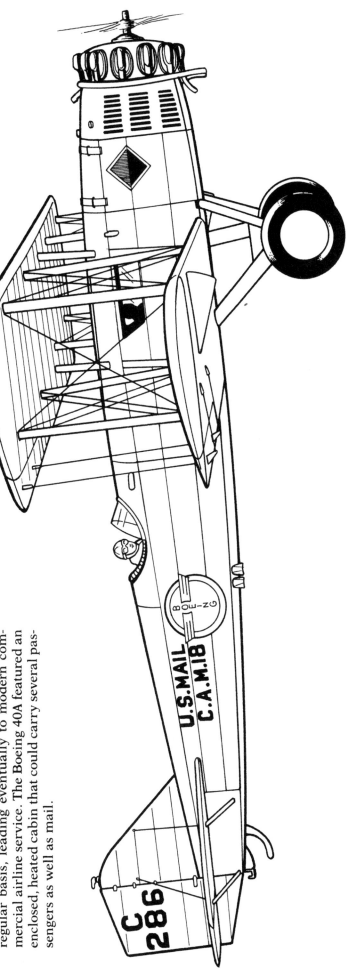
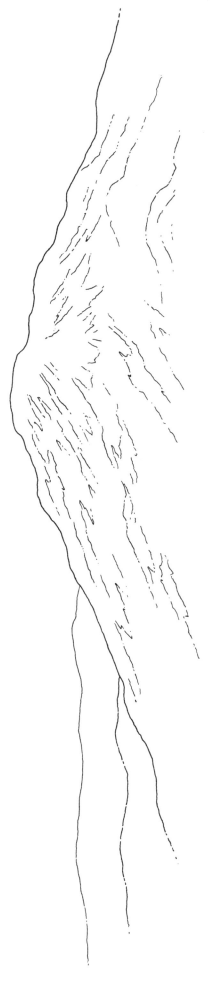

26. Ford Tri-Motor "Tin Goose" (1926). This high-wing monoplane transport, first manufactured in 1926, was an early mainstay of American commercial aviation, earning the affectionate nickname "Tin Goose" (analogous to Ford's "Tin Lizzie"). Its lightweight, all-metal construction (wingspan 70 feet, length 40 feet) and three 200 hp. radial engines gave it improved payload capacity and reliability.

The Ford "Tin Goose" carried a two-man crew and 11 to 14 passengers seated in wicker chairs. There was also room for several hundred pounds of mail. Its cruising speed was 107 mph. and its range 570 miles. Henry Ford soon left the aircraft-manufacturing business, but many of his sturdy Tri-Motors remained in service for decades.

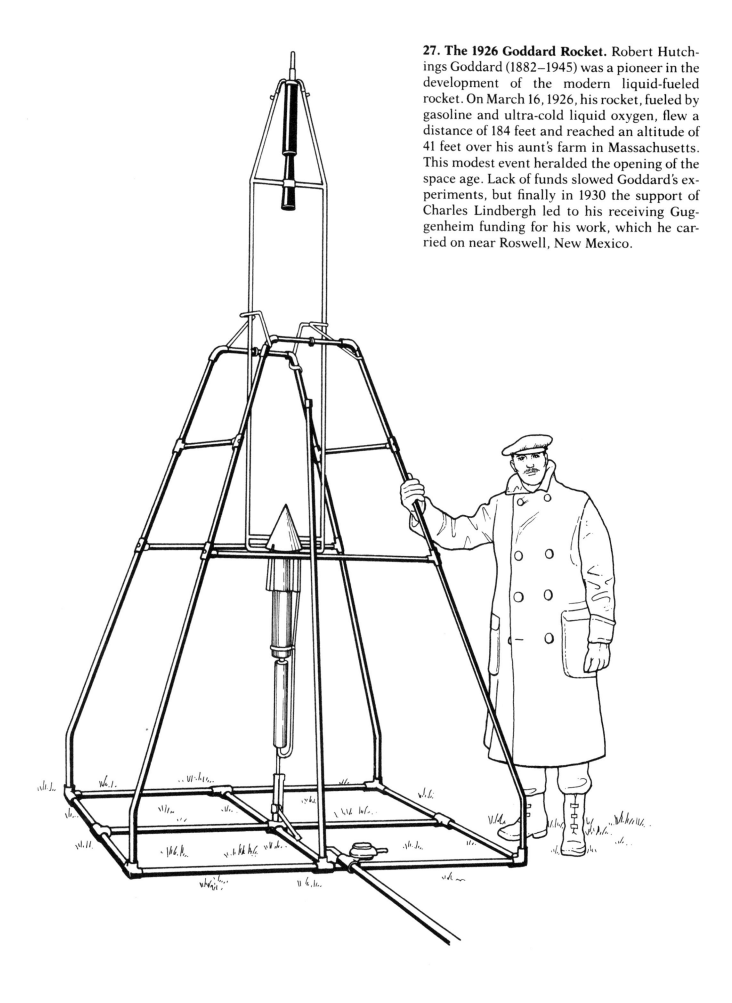

27. The 1926 Goddard Rocket. Robert Hutchings Goddard (1882–1945) was a pioneer in the development of the modern liquid-fueled rocket. On March 16, 1926, his rocket, fueled by gasoline and ultra-cold liquid oxygen, flew a distance of 184 feet and reached an altitude of 41 feet over his aunt's farm in Massachusetts. This modest event heralded the opening of the space age. Lack of funds slowed Goddard's experiments, but finally in 1930 the support of Charles Lindbergh led to his receiving Guggenheim funding for his work, which he carried on near Roswell, New Mexico.

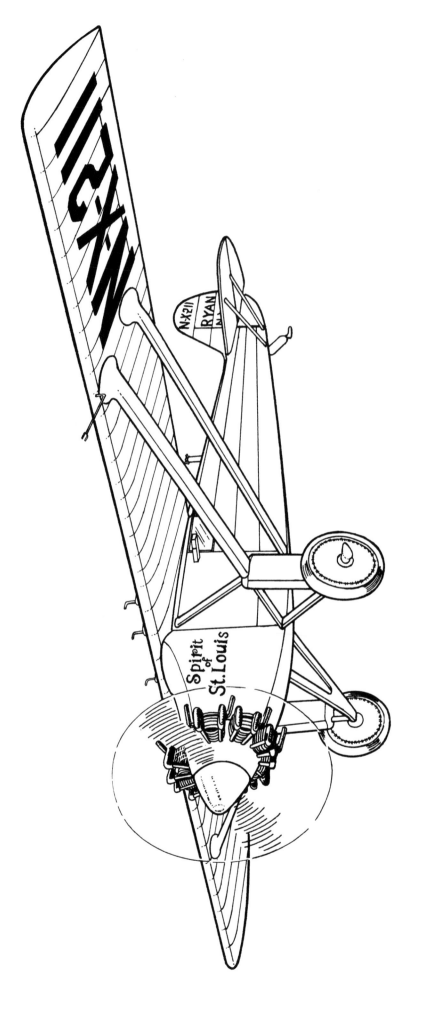

28. Ryan NYP *Spirit of St. Louis* (1927). On May 20–21, 1927, a young airmail pilot named Charles A. Lindbergh became the first to fly nonstop from New York to Paris. His was also the first solo trans-Atlantic flight, and it won him the $25,000 Orteig prize. Lindbergh was hailed as a hero on two continents, and his feat remains the most celebrated of all solo airplane flights. His plane, the *Spirit of St. Louis,* became as famous as its pilot. The Ryan NYP aircraft was specially designed by Donald A. Hall with Lindbergh's participation and produced by the Ryan Company of San Diego in only 60 days. Its wingspan was 46 feet, it was 27 feet 8 inches long, and it was powered by a Wright radial engine of advanced design rated at 220 hp.

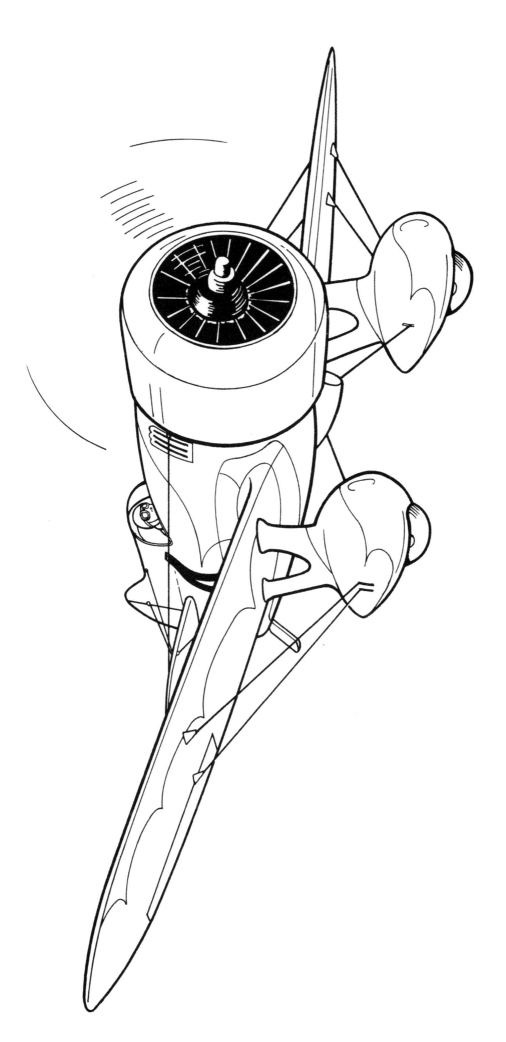

29. Gee Bee Model Z "Super Sportster." The Model Z was the first of the series of famous Gee Bee racers. The Gordon Bennett races and the Schneider Cup races offered prizes and provided a showcase for new aircraft and increasingly powerful engines. Many of the developments first seen in these Gee Bee and other racers were applied to the fighter aircraft of World War II.

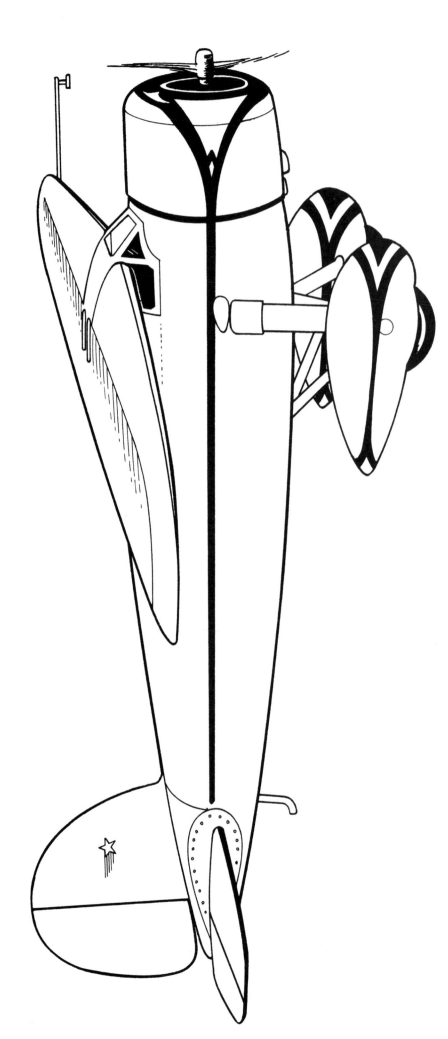

30. Lockheed Vega (1927). During the 1920s and 1930s many now-famous aircraft manufacturers began their operations. The first product of the Lockheed Corporation was its structurally and aerodynamically advanced high-wing monoplane of 1927, designed by John K. Northrop. Later-model Vegas were among the first to employ streamlined long-chord engine cowling. In 1932, Amelia Earhart, flying a Lockheed Vega, became the first woman to make a solo trans-Atlantic flight. In the early 1930s, other records were set by Wiley Post and other aviators flying Lockheed Vegas.

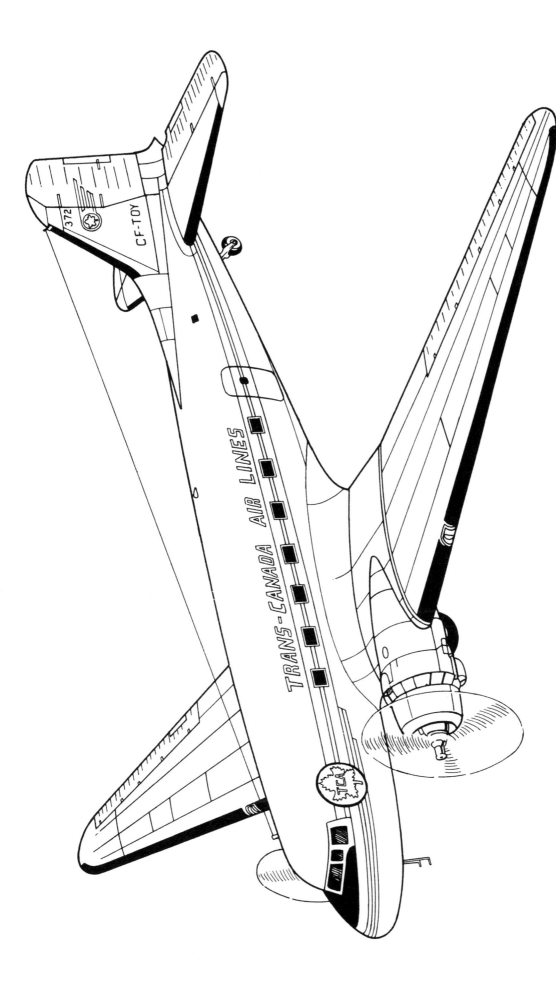

31. Douglas DC-3 (1935). Commercial air transport came into its own in the mid-1930s, particularly with the introduction of the Douglas DC-3 in 1935. This revolutionary airliner incorporated every advanced engineering feature of its day and could carry up to 21 passengers in a heated, soundproofed cabin. The 64-foot-5¾-inch-long plane (wingspan 95 feet 6¼ inches) cruised effortlessly at 180 mph. at an altitude of 8,000 to 10,000 feet, and could fly coast-to-coast with only three stops. Thousands of DC-3s were soon flying for airliners in several countries, and modified versions saw wartime service. Many overhauled DC-3s are still in service today.

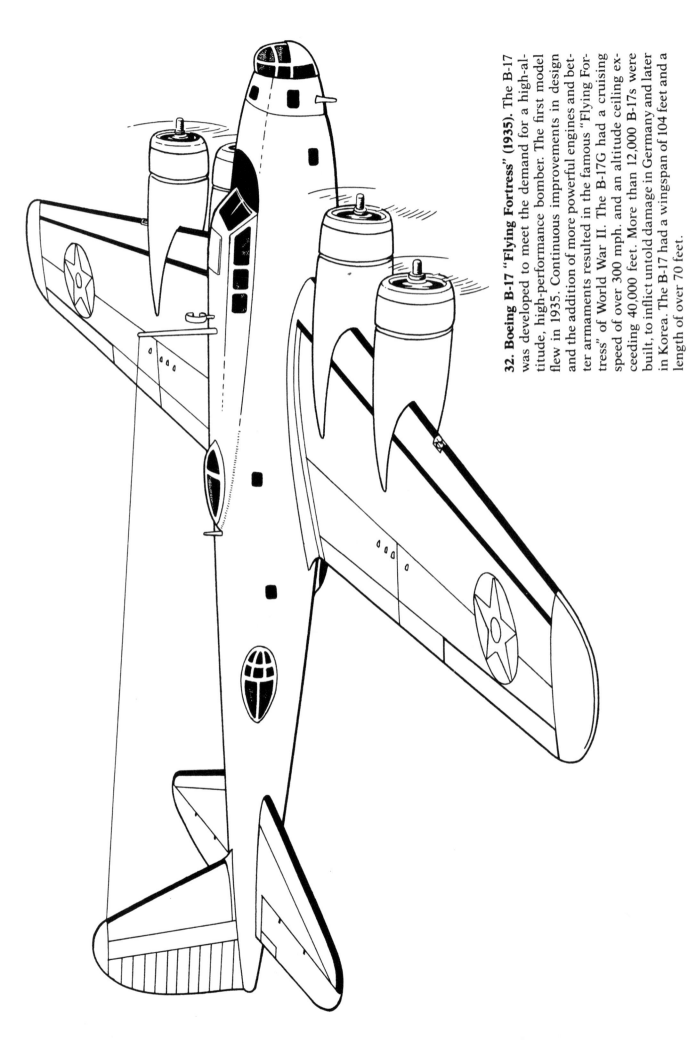

32. Boeing B-17 "Flying Fortress" (1935). The B-17 was developed to meet the demand for a high-altitude, high-performance bomber. The first model flew in 1935. Continuous improvements in design and the addition of more powerful engines and better armaments resulted in the famous "Flying Fortress" of World War II. The B-17G had a cruising speed of over 300 mph. and an altitude ceiling exceeding 40,000 feet. More than 12,000 B-17s were built, to inflict untold damage in Germany and later in Korea. The B-17 had a wingspan of 104 feet and a length of over 70 feet.

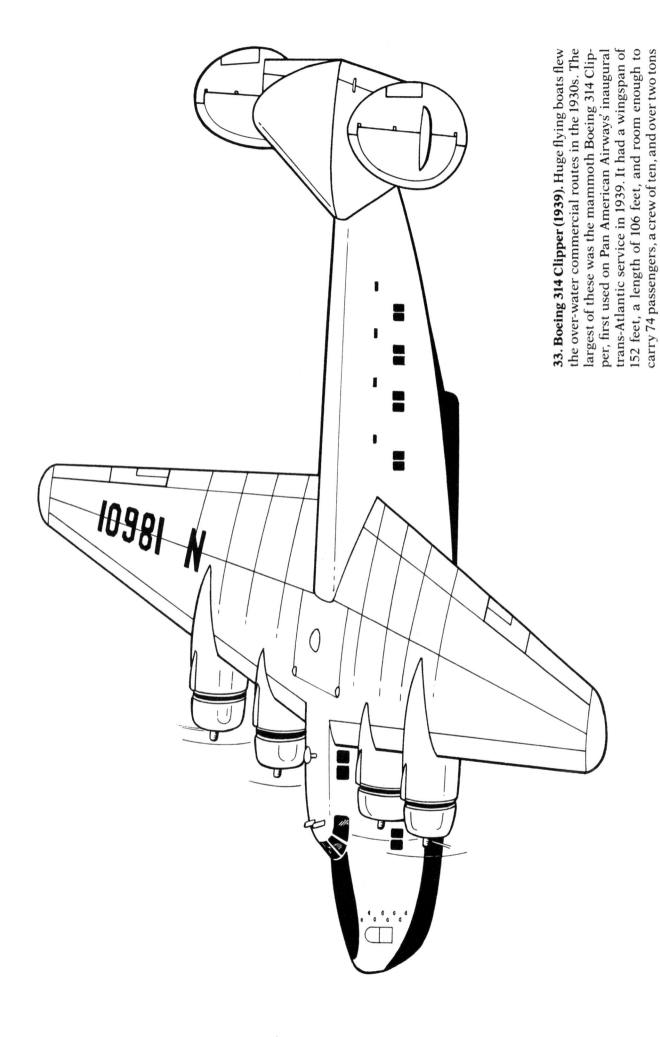

33. Boeing 314 Clipper (1939). Huge flying boats flew the over-water commercial routes in the 1930s. The largest of these was the mammoth Boeing 314 Clipper, first used on Pan American Airways' inaugural trans-Atlantic service in 1939. It had a wingspan of 152 feet, a length of 106 feet, and room enough to carry 74 passengers, a crew of ten, and over two tons of mail at a cruising speed of 175 mph. for over 3,000 miles without landing. It featured a dining salon with full-service kitchen.

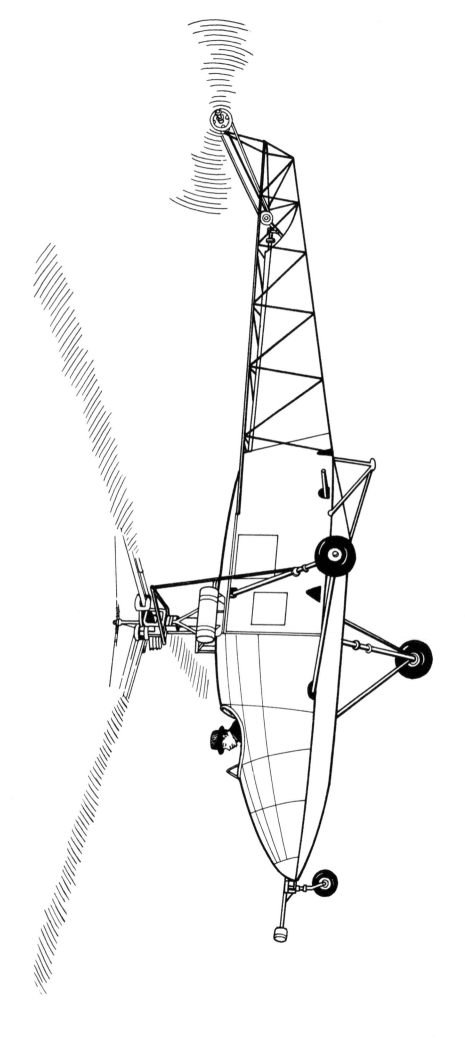

34. Vought-Sikorsky VS-300 (1939). Although Igor Sikorsky (1889–1972) built his first helicopter in Russia in 1909, his early experiments were not entirely successful, and he began to devote himself to designing conventional aircraft. He emigrated to the U.S. in 1919 and in the 1930s returned to his experiments with helicopter designs, finally overcoming problems of control in 1939 by introduction of variable-pitch rotor blades and a small tail rotor. Sikorsky was awarded a military contract in 1940. Production of the VS-300 and subsequent variations soon followed, paving the way for all modern helicopter development.

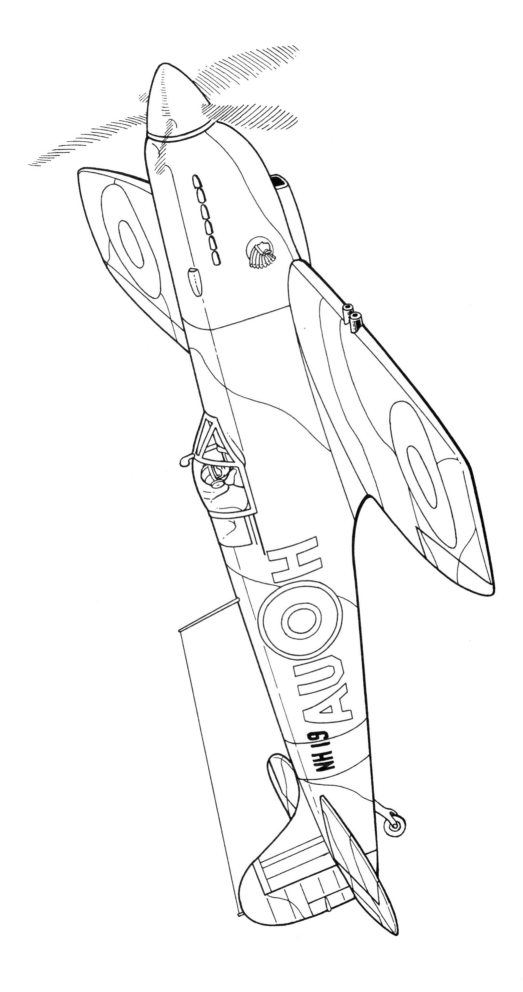

35. Vickers Supermarine "Spitfire." The origins of this famous World War II British fighter can be traced back to the Supermarine racing seaplanes of the late 1920s. The first "Spitfire" eight-gun fighter flew in March 1936. During the Battle of Britain and afterwards, successive variations of this beautifully designed plane became famous for their maneuverability and performance at high altitude. The "Spitfire" MK XXII had a maximum speed of 454 mph.

36. Whittle Jet Engine. The English military aviator and inventor Frank Whittle first proposed the use of jet propulsion for aircraft in 1928. His engine design was first patented in 1930 and tested in succeeding years. The Whittle engine used a centrifugal compressor to compress air and spin it out over fins on a rapidly rotating disc. This engine powered the first British jet, the Gloster E.28/39, in May 1941. Meanwhile jet-powered airplanes had also been developed in Germany, foreshadowing the replacement of all propeller-driven fighter planes by jets. For his work on jet engines Frank Whittle received a knighthood and an award of £100,000.

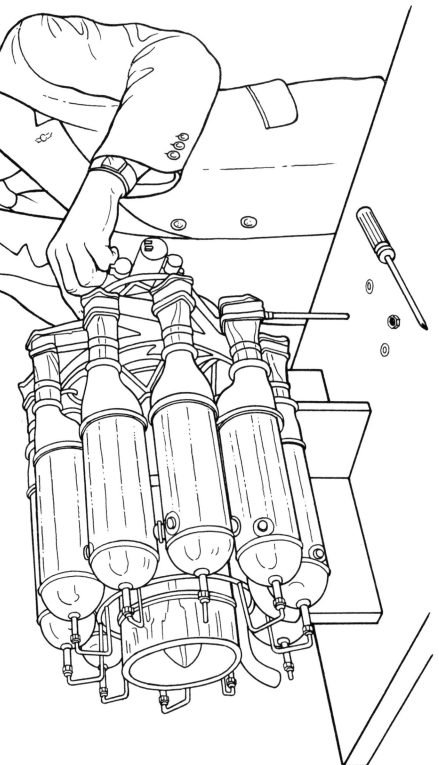

37. V-2 Rocket (1944). The Germans also pioneered in rocket development following the theoretical work of Hermann Oberth in the 1920s. Thereafter the development of rocket-powered guided missiles progressed rapidly in Germany, eventuating in the V-2 rocket. This remarkable 47-foot-long rocket (diameter 5½ feet) could transport its one-ton warhead to a predetermined target 200 miles from its launch point, at a phenomenal speed of some five times that of sound. The Germans launched over 4,000 of these formidable weapons against Allied targets in the last few months of World War II.

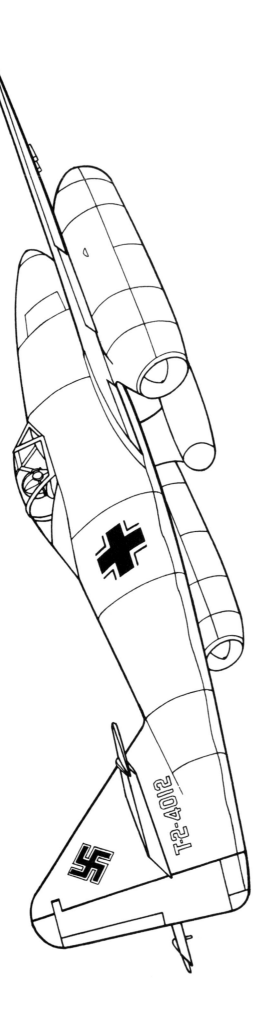

38. Messerschmitt Me 262 A (1945). The German Messerschmitt Me 262 A was the first jet fighter to participate in combat. Design work on jet-powered aircraft began in Germany in 1938 and the prototype of the Me 262 flew in 1942. Production was delayed by design changes and Allied bombing. Only a few of the 1,433 built actually participated in air combat. This high-performance fighter was powered by twin turbojet engines and had a maximum speed of 540 mph., making it far faster than any propeller-driven plane.

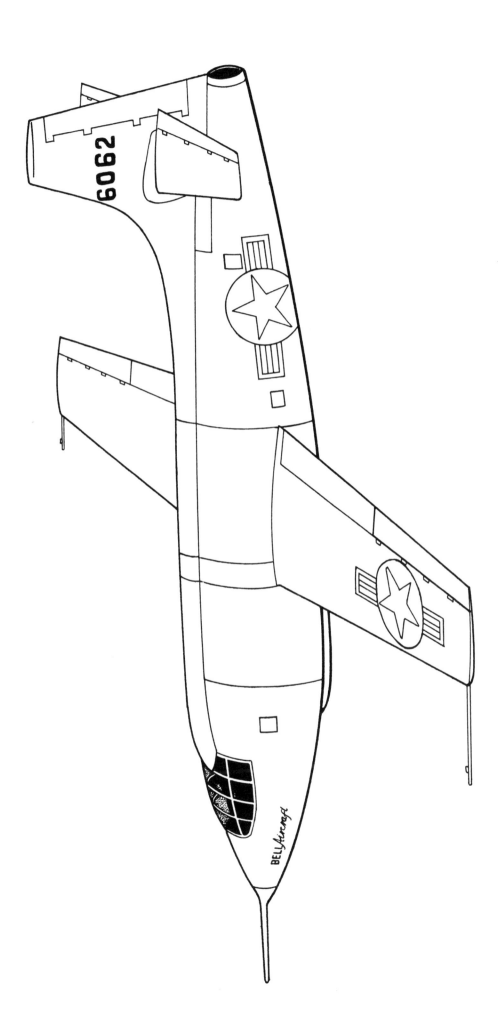

39. Bell X-1 (1947). On October 14, 1947, the Bell X-1 became the first manned aircraft to exceed the speed of sound. The rocket-propelled research aircraft was piloted by Captain Charles E. Yeager of the U.S. Air Force. Tests continued and on December 12, 1953, the X-1A reached a speed of 1,650 mph. The X-1 was 31 feet long and had a wingspan of only 28 feet.

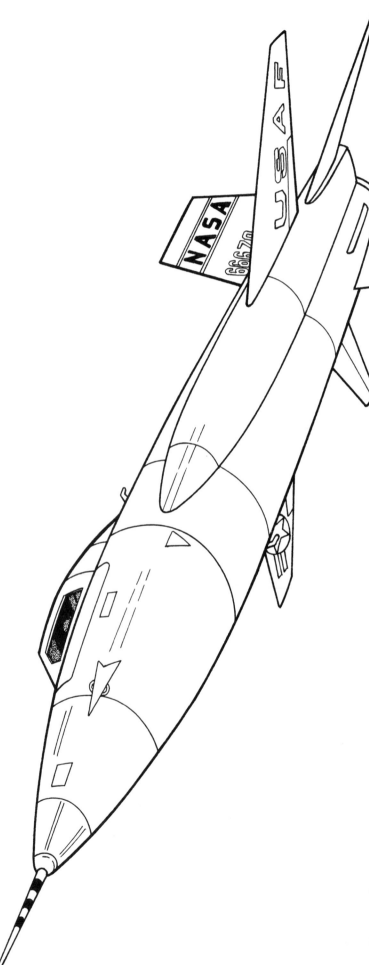

40. North American X-15. The X-15 rocket-powered research aircraft was first tested in September 1959. Over the following nine years it made 159 manned flights. It flew at record-breaking speeds reaching 4,500 mph. and at record-breaking altitudes of over 350,000 feet (67 miles). The data learned from the X-15 program contributed to the development of the manned space programs of the late 1960s and 1970s and to the Space Shuttle program. The X-15 was 52 feet long; its wingspan was only 22 feet.

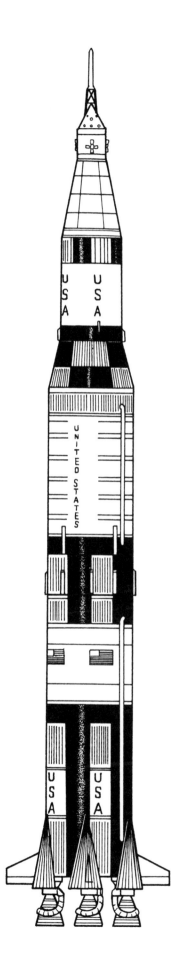

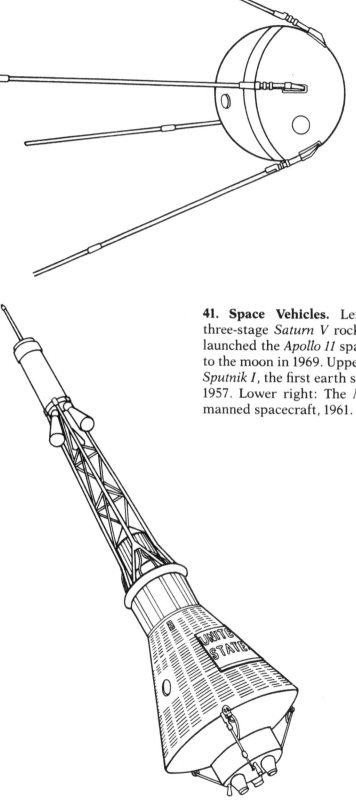

41. Space Vehicles. Left: The three-stage *Saturn V* rocket that launched the *Apollo 11* spacecraft to the moon in 1969. Upper right: *Sputnik I*, the first earth satellite, 1957. Lower right: The *Mercury* manned spacecraft, 1961.

42. *Apollo 11* Lunar Module *Eagle* (1969). After achieving lunar orbit, the two-man landing module of the *Apollo 11*, the *Eagle*, carrying astronauts Neil A. Armstrong and Edwin E. Aldrin, Jr., was separated from the *Apollo*'s command and service modules. It then descended to the surface of the moon on a historic moment on July 20, 1969. When the crew was ready to return to the command module, the upper half, or ascent stage, containing the crew cabin, was separated and took off, leaving the lower half, or descent stage, on the lunar surface. The entire module was 23 feet high.

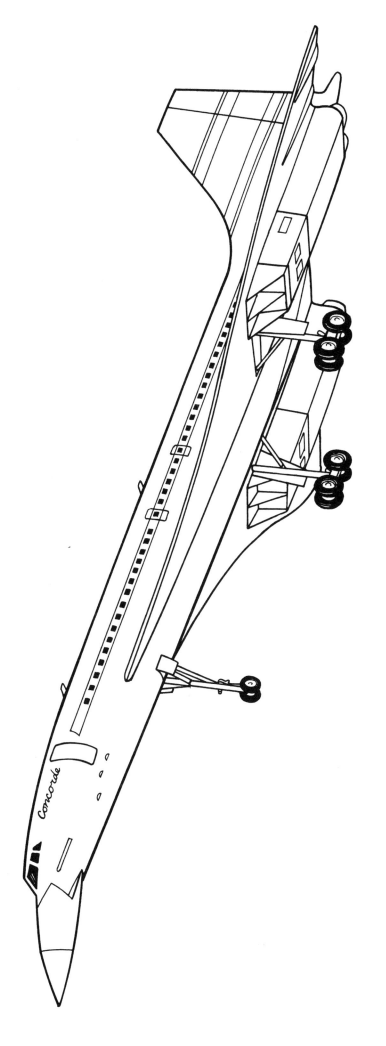

43. Concorde Supersonic Transport (1969). The Concorde was developed and produced under a joint agreement between the British Aircraft Corporation, Ltd., and Sud-Aviation, France. The prototype of this supersonic transport flew in 1969. The Concorde is now in service on major long-distance routes. It can carry up to 128 passengers at a maximum cruising speed of 1,450 mph. The nose of the Concorde is dropped hydraulically to improve visibility on takeoff and landing.

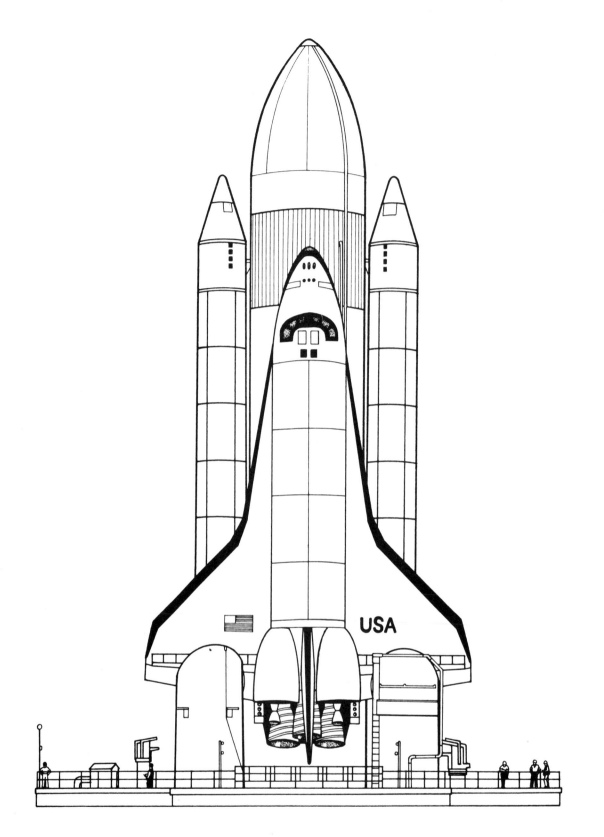

44. NASA Space Shuttle. The NASA (National Aeronautics and Space Administration) Space Shuttle was conceived as a reusable spacecraft for ferrying satellites and crews of observers into orbit. The 122-foot-long shuttle (wingspan 78 feet) is launched vertically by giant booster rockets but returns and lands on a runway as a conventional aircraft (without power, however). It goes into orbit at a height of 115 miles. Five orbiters were eventually built. The first, the *Enterprise*, was a test vehicle, flown first in 1977. Four other orbiters—the *Columbia*, the *Challenger*, the *Discovery*, and the *Atlantis*—actually carried passengers on missions in space. On January 28, 1986, the NASA space program suffered a tragic setback when the Space Shuttle *Challenger* and all personnel aboard were destroyed in an explosion—a chastening reminder of the continuing hazards of pioneering flight.